# A·Q·U·A·M·A·S·T·E·R ™

Derek Lambert • Graham Quick

# POND PLANTS

## BOWTIE
### P·R·E·S·S®

A Division of BowTie, Inc.
Irvine, California

First published in the USA and Canada by BowTie Press®
A Division of BowTie, Inc.
3 Burroughs
Irvine, CA 92618
www.bowtiepress.com

Originally Published in 2006
© 2006 Interpet Publishing
Vincent Lane, Dorking, Surrey
RH4 3YX, England

Library of Congress Cataloging-in-Publication Data

Lambert, Derek.
  Pond plants / by Derek Lambert, Graham
Quick, and Philip Swindells.
        p. cm.— (Aquamaster)
  ISBN 1-931993-81-5
  1.  Aquatic plants. 2.  Pond plants. I. Quick,
Graham. II. Swindells,Philip. III. Title. IV. Series.

  SB423.L2647 2006
  635.9'674—dc22

2006019996

**Created and compiled:** Ideas into Print,
Claydon, Suffolk, IP6 0AB, England
**Design and prepress:** Phil Kay Design, Elmdon,
Saffron Walden, Essex CB11 4LT, England
**Computer graphics:** Phil Holmes and
Stuart Watkinson
**Photography:** Geoffrey Rogers and Neil
Sutherland © Interpet Publishing (Also see Picture
credits, page 96)
**Production management:** Consortium,
Poslingford, Suffolk CO10 8RA, England
**Print production:** Sino Publishing House Ltd.,
Hong Kong

Printed and bound in China
10 9 8 7 6 5 4 3 2 1

**Consultant: Sue Westlake-Guy** is one of the
founders of a leading aquatic plant nursery. She
has more than thirty years experience in growing
and supplying water plants for wholesale and
retail sale.

CONTENTS

# Contents

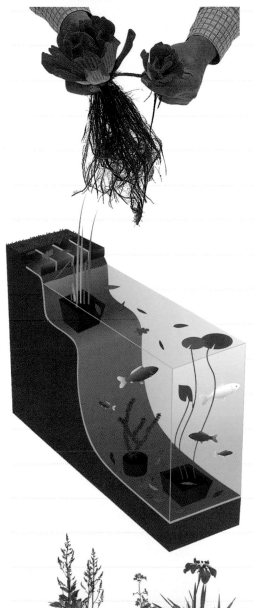

# *Using pond plants*

The pond plants that surround and live in the pond play a vital role in its ecosystem. Species range from moisture-loving plants, which would normally be found 12 in (30 cm) or more away from the edge; to the marginals, which have their roots and part of their stems underwater; to true aquatic plants. Each group contains plants that are happy in more than one environment: many moisture-loving plants can live partially submerged for periods of time, and marginals can tolerate drier conditions. They have to do this in the wild, because ponds and rivers rise and fall depending on rainfall.

## THE ROLE OF PLANTS IN AND AROUND THE POND

### Floating plants

These provide cover in a new pond until the deep water plants are established. They offer instant cover and shade for fish and reduce the amount of sunlight reaching the water.

▶ *Floating plant roots are a haven for young fish.*

### Deep water aquatics and water lilies

These offer the main shade in the established pond and grow in the deeper water where other plants would not survive. The large leaves, especially those of water lilies, offer safe areas for fish to rest and hide away from predators above.

▼ *There are water lilies to suit every size of garden pond.*

### Oxygenators

These are the first plants to go into a new pond and offer shade for the fish and food if needed. As they grow quickly, they reduce the nitrate levels and thus help to check algae growth.

◀ *Planting oxygenators in baskets makes it easier to remove excess growth.*

## THE ROLE OF SUNLIGHT

For best results, pond plants require a position in full, uninterrupted sunlight, even though this is conducive to a proliferation of green, water-discoloring algae. In such a situation, the plants will flourish and compete with the algae, the submerged oxygenating plants using the dissolved nutrients in the water and the floating aquatics reducing the light falling directly beneath the water surface. Together, they make it difficult for primitive plant life, such as algae, to thrive.

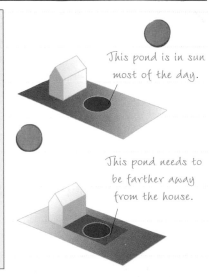

This pond is in sun most of the day.

This pond needs to be farther away from the house.

### Marginal plants

These provide more than just color and form, although this is their main role. They also absorb minerals from the water and create shade and a convenient route for the wildlife to access the pond. Emerging dragonflies climb the stems of tall marginals to dry their new wings.

▲ Hostas are superb for boggy ground. Flowers are a bonus to the stunning leaves.

▲ Houttuynia cordata 'Chameleon' provides a vivid splash of poolside color.

### Bog plants

These plants thrive in the transition zone between the pond and dry land. In natural ponds, the plants in this moist environment hold back the banks with their roots. Around a pond, they can provide color and interest in every season.

USING POND PLANTS

## Planting zones

With such a large array of pond plants to choose from, it can be difficult to know where to start. For this reason, it is often better to begin by drawing a planting plan. There are four distinct areas to stock: the pond surround, planted with normal garden plants in keeping with the style of pond you are creating; the bog garden area (unlined earth) for moisture-loving plants; marginal shelves, which are completely submersed; and finally, deep water areas, where plants such as water lilies will flourish. There is a selection of plants for each area, and you should make a list of those you intend to buy.

▼ *Marsh marigolds are one of the earliest-flowering marginal aquatics, adding welcome color.*

▲ *All areas of the pond are enhanced by a well-balanced planting plan. Make one early on.*

▶ *The beautiful bog primulas thrive in damp soil by the pond. Plant them in groups for a stunning display. They seed freely, so look out for new seedlings, and space these out as soon as they are big enough to transplant.*

## THE PLANTING ZONES OF A POND

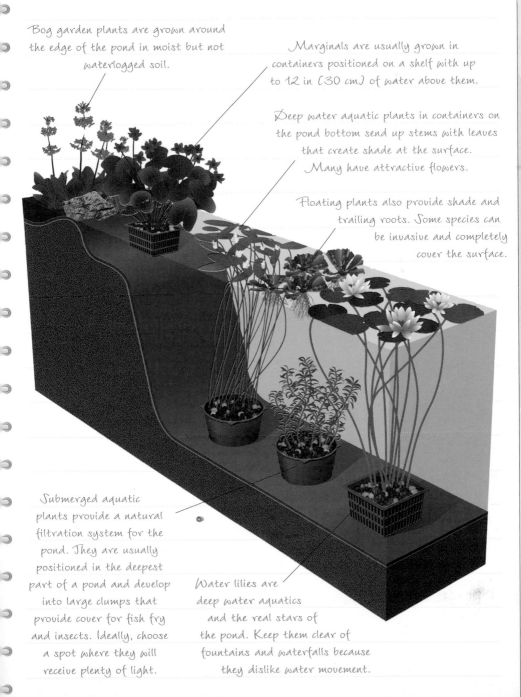

Bog garden plants are grown around the edge of the pond in moist but not waterlogged soil.

Marginals are usually grown in containers positioned on a shelf with up to 12 in (30 cm) of water above them.

Deep water aquatic plants in containers on the pond bottom send up stems with leaves that create shade at the surface. Many have attractive flowers.

Floating plants also provide shade and trailing roots. Some species can be invasive and completely cover the surface.

Submerged aquatic plants provide a natural filtration system for the pond. They are usually positioned in the deepest part of a pond and develop into large clumps that provide cover for fish fry and insects. Ideally, choose a spot where they will receive plenty of light.

Water lilies are deep water aquatics and the real stars of the pond. Keep them clear of fountains and waterfalls because they dislike water movement.

# Planting strategy

Start by planting two principal areas: the deep water area and the space around the pond. Most important of all are the deep water species—water lilies, other deep water aquatic plants, and oxygenators—and you can buy these as soon as all danger of frost has passed. The other area to plant at an early stage is the one around the pond that features large plants that may take a long time to achieve a mature look. Once the main structure is in place, you can plant the marginals and finally the bog plants.

◀ *Oxygenators should be planted as early as possible in a new pond's life. These should be grown in containers and carefully lowered into position.*

*\* Some people recommend placing a layer of soil across the liner for oxygenators to root into. Unfortunately, this rarely works, as the more vigorous plants usually take over and smother the more desirable ones, producing an uncontrollable green jungle in the pond.*

## THE AREA AROUND THE POND

Here, there should be sufficient plants to create an attractive display but not so many that they are cramped and have little or no room for growth. Once again, always plant in groups of species rather than introduce the odd individual here and there. If you intend to feature large plants, bear in mind that many shrubs take a few years to establish, particularly if you start with small plants. Around a formal pond or one that is part of a patio, you can use containers filled with annual plants to create a changing display.

▶ *Rheum makes a handsome feature plant, growing to 10 ft (3 m) in height. In spring, the new leaf buds of the red rheum* (Rheum palmatum) *are a vivid red. Mature plants have red or creamy-white flowers.*

*◀ Goldfish are the classic pond fish, adding welcome color and movement.*

## THE ROLE OF FISH

Fish can play an essential role in a pond, even if you are focused on the plants. They keep many aquatic insect pests under control and eliminate mosquito larvae. However, if there are too many fish, they may start to damage the plants or add excessive nutrients to the water with their natural waste. Allow no more than 18 in (45 cm) total length of fish (excluding tails) for each 3.5 ft² (1 m²) of water surface area.

## BOG GARDEN PLANTS

In the bog garden area, you have a large selection of plants, to choose from. Many of them can be invasive, so you may have to grow them in containers sunk into the waterlogged soil. A dressing of bark chips will disguise the tops of the containers. In the area closest to the water, try to select plants that will grow over the edge of the pond. Creeping jenny *(Lysimachia nummularia)* and water forget-me-not *(Myosotis scorpioides)* are particularly good for this and soon form a clump that grows right down into the water.

*▼ A bog garden should be a natural adjunct to the pond, the water dampening the soil and helping to sustain the plants.*

# How many plants?

Plant stocking levels will vary depending on the type of pond you have created. You must also take into account the amount of light and how much water movement there is going to be in any particular area. Although there are no hard and fast rules about how many plants you can have in a pond, the ideal seems to be that one-third of the deep water surface area should be covered in floating plants and the floating leaves of deep water aquatic plants, such as water lilies. Another third can be left open, while the final third will have oxygenators growing in containers on the pond bottom.

▲ *This pond has the ideal proportion of surface cover provided by water lily leaves. Oxygenating plants occupy a further third of the pond base, and the remaining areas are left without plants.*

◀ *Formal ponds tend to look better when the visible planting is kept to a minimum, but you should increase the number of oxygenators to compensate for the reduced number of other plants.*

## WATER LILIES

It is theoretically possible to cover your pond with water lily leaves. The problem is that part of the pond may have too much water movement, which water lilies do not like. Secondly, there may not be sufficient light for them to flower well. Finally, the abundance of water lily foliage will prevent light reaching any oxygenators growing below the water surface.

▲ *Water lilies are the most popular water plants with floating leaves.*

▲ *In wildlife ponds with no fish, it does not matter if little open water remains, although you will want some clear areas so that you can see any amphibians or other wildlife under the water.*

▼ *In the shallow water areas where marginals are growing you can place as many containers as you have room for. It is a good idea to have clusters of the same plant rather than single specimens dotted here and there. This can be achieved either by putting several plants of the same species together in one basket or by placing several baskets next to each other. Baskets are available in various sizes.*

HOW MANY PLANTS?

# *Buying pond plants*

With your plant list at hand, you can start to visit garden centers and aquatic plant dealers. You will probably buy your plants in batches, not only to spread the cost but also because you are unlikely to find all the plants you want in one place. Choose your plants with care. Whatever their size, beware of cheap offers. Often, these are either inferior varieties or starved, checked, diseased, or very young plants. Paying a fair price for really good plants is an investment that will grow in value year by year.

## WHAT TO LOOK FOR

Nowadays, most pond plants are supplied in containers. They should look fresh and not forced into growth. They should not have been established in their pots so long that they have become stunted and jaded. They may recover if their roots are teased out and trimmed, but this can often take the whole season.

## MAIL-ORDER PLANTS

If you are looking for slightly unusual varieties or are seeking plants in quantity, consider buying by mail order. Mail-order plants are available throughout the year. To create something of a display in the first year, buy freshly sprouting plants early in the season.

▼ *This is a plant to avoid—starved and in an inadequate container and competing with a mass of seedling weeds.*

* Many aquatic centers stock only the plants that are in flower at the time; choosing just these would provide a flowering display that is over in a month. Choose plants that spread their flowering over the season for long-term interest.

▲ *This is a good plant to buy. It has healthy foliage, a full-size flower, and a well-presented container topped with gravel.*

▶ *Submerged aquatics are less likely to be grown in pots. The majority are sold in bunches fastened together with a strip of lead. The foliage of underwater plants should always be fresh and show no signs of browning or other discoloration.*

*\* Caution! Many states have laws that can ban the use of certain plants. Check before purchasing.*

◀ *Always read up on a plant before buying. Many labels give only limited information or skim over problems such as how invasive a plant may be. Terms such as* vigorous *or* fast-growing *often mean that the plant can become a rampant weed!*

*\* A large number of aquatic plant flowers are yellow, so look out for other colors and a variety of leaf shapes.*

## SELECTING A WATER LILY

Before choosing a water lily, be sure to take into account the size of the pond, the water depth, and the amount of sun it receives. Look for rich green leaves (not brown slimy ones) with no yellowing at the edges. The crown should be hard, as this is where the plant stores its food during winter. The roots should be growing through the sides of the basket; newly potted ones are not the best buys because they can take some time to settle down again. Good retailers display the plants in shallow tanks at least 12 in (30 cm) deep. Avoid water lilies kept in plastic boxes but not in water. These can dry out and even get mold on them, from which they rarely recover.

▲ *These water lilies in containers are displayed with adequate water depth, allowing the leaves to float naturally.*

# *Baskets and mixes*

...dern pond or under any circumstances where plants need to be separated ...ntrolled, be sure to use aquatic planting baskets. These containers permit the healthy exchange of gases that would be restricted by a solid pot. Plastic baskets are available in a range of shapes and sizes, and those with micromesh sides prevent soil spillage into the water. There is no need to line micromesh baskets, but you may want to anchor the bottoms with rocks before planting. Use good-quality aquatic soil and not peat-based potting mixes, which float in the pond and release a brown color.

## PLANTING BASKETS

Planting baskets are available in all shapes and sizes.

Planting baskets with fine holes do not need fiber or foam liners to retain the soil.

Flexible containers are an excellent alternative to rigid baskets.

Wide-mesh plastic baskets need a liner to stop the soil from leaching out into the water.

▲ Flexible containers are easy to mold into odd corners of the pond to produce tighter clumps of plants, and they restrict the fast-growing plant roots. Other plus points are that they will sit on uneven surfaces without rocking, and the soft material cannot damage the liner.

* Planting baskets are generally tapered in shape, which helps with the balance of the plants. In high winds, tall reeds or rushes growing in baskets can easily topple over. Plants that are constantly retrieved from the water never develop satisfactorily.

◀ *When planting a selection of aquatic plants in the same basket, do not mix strong-growing varieties with weak ones, otherwise the weak ones will be overrun. These curved baskets are ideal for placing on the marginal shelf.*

*You can buy specially formulated soil for use in aquatic planting baskets.*

## FEEDING PLANTS

The easiest way to feed pond plants is to introduce specially manufactured aquatic feed tablets or sachets of slow-release feed to the planted baskets following the manufacturer's instructions.

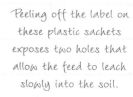

*Peeling off the label on these plastic sachets exposes two holes that allow the feed to leach slowly into the soil.*

*These are slow-release feed tablets. Simply bury one or two in the soil close to the plant roots.*

## USING GARDEN SOIL

Instead of aquatic mix, you could use soil from a neglected part of the garden (as long as it is not alkaline or treated with weed killer). Do not add general garden fertilizers as they are water soluble and will dissolve in the pond, encouraging algae and green water. Use a sieve to remove sticks, stones, and water-polluting organic material.

BASKETS AND MIXES

# *Potting oxygenators*

Submerged plants, also called oxygenators, help to keep the pond clean and healthy because, like all plants, they use nitrate as food and so remove it from the water. Some large clumps should be included in any pond. While most submerged aquatic plants will be only partly visible beneath the water, some do send up stems or flowers above the surface. These make them particularly useful for positioning at the pond edge, where they help to soften the barrier between the water and the land.

▶ *Oxygenators are usually sold in bunches. Always remove the lead strip that is wrapped around the stems as this can cause the plants to rot off just above the strip. Also, it is best to avoid any heavy metals in the pond as they pose a possible health hazard to the fish.*

\* Spacing out the stems creates a large thicket of plants that will receive enough light and nutrients for healthy growth.

Remove this lead strip before planting.

## PLANTING OXYGENATORS

This is *Elodea canadensis*, a vigorous oxygenator.

1 Submerged plants will grow much more successfully if you separate the cuttings and plant them individually.

2 Carefully unwrap the packing material. Using sharp scissors, trim the base of the stems, cutting above any damaged areas.

## COMMON OXYGENATING PLANTS

*Callitriche hermaphroditica*—Autumn starwort
*Ceratophyllum demersum*—Hornwort
*Eleocharis acicularis*—Neele spikerush
*Elodea canadensis*—Canadian pondweed
*Fontinalis antipyretica*—Willow moss
*Hottonia palustris*—Water violet
*Lagarosiphon major (Elodea crispa)*—Fish weed
*Myriophyllum spicatum*—Spiked milfoil
*Myriophyllum verticillatum*—Whorled water milfoil
*Potamogeton crispus*—Curled pondweed
*Ranunculus aquatilis*—Water crowfoot
For more details, see pages 54–57.

▲ *Hornwort is an excellent oxygenator and very hardy.*

3 Using a stick, make holes in the aquatic planting mixture at 2-in (5-cm) intervals. Carefully insert a stem into each hole.

4 Backfill with mix and firm each stem into place with your fingers. Cover the surface with a 1-in (2.5-cm) layer of aquarium gravel.

5 Water the pot thoroughly before placing it at the bottom of the pond. The stems will send out side shoots, creating a mass of oxygenating plants.

POTTING OXYGENATORS

# The role of floating plants

Floating plants provide welcome shade for fish, reduce the amount of light reaching the water, and use up nitrates, thus reducing the likelihood of an algal bloom. Many also produce attractive flowers and have interesting leaf shapes. Floating plants provide instant cover for new ponds until the deep water plants have grown enough to create shade. Most grow quickly and need regular thinning out to prevent them from shading the submerged plants they are supposed to be helping. A few are not hardy in any but the warmest climates and need protection in winter. Alternatively, replace them yearly.

▲ *The fine trailing roots of* Salvinia natans *(floating fern) provide an excellent refuge for young fish.*

## POPULAR FLOATING PLANTS

*Eichhornia crassipes*—Water hyacinth
*Hydrocharis morsus-ranae*—Frogbit
*Pistia stratiotes*—Water lettuce
*Salvinia auriculata/natans*—Floating fern
*Stratiotes aloides*—Water soldier
*Trapa natans*—Water chestnut
*Utricularia vulgaris*—Greater bladderwort
For more details, see pages 58–59.

* Beneath the water, the trailing roots of floating plants provide living quarters for aquatic insect life and a haven for spawning fish and emerging fry.

## POTENTIAL PEST SPECIES

Some floating plants can become a major problem in ponds; duckweed and azolla are the main offenders. However careful you are to wash duckweed off new introductions, most established ponds have a covering of it and it should be netted out regularly.

Left to its own devices, azolla can cover the pond surface and build up into a thick layer. When winter comes, most of the layer dies off and starts to rot, causing serious water quality problems. Once again, net out large quantities of the plant every week.

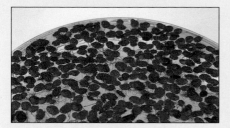

▲ *Duckweed* (Lemna minor) *thrives in slow-flowing or still water.*

▶ *Do not allow azolla* (Azolla filiculoides) *to cover the whole pond.*

## PARROT'S FEATHER

Parrot's feather *(Myriophyllum aquaticum)* is a South American plant that will spread rapidly, forming a dense floating mat over the water surface. This prevents light getting into the water, kills off submerged oxygenators, and destroys the underwater habitat for amphibians, insects, and fish. Control it by removing plant mats with a rake and composting them. A good alternative is *Myriophyllum spicatum*.

◀ *Here* Myriophyllum aquaticum *is spreading across a pond. Avoid releasing this rampant plant into natural waterways.*

# Potting marginals

arginal plants grow at pond margins, where the water level fluctuates
rainfall and the time of year. This means that the plants are able to cope
with so variation in water depth, but most have an ideal planting depth that you
should take into account. At one extreme, this will mean placing the crown just above
the waterline, while at the other it should be well below the surface, with just the foliage
showing above. Most garden centers label their plants so that you can make sure you
plant them at the correct depth.

## POTTING A MARGINAL

1
Carefully remove the plant from its old container.

Choose a suitable basket for repotting. Plastic micromesh planters are ideal as they do not need lining before you fill them with aquatic planting mixture.

2 Trim off any damaged stems. This is *Juncus effusus* 'Spiralis'. Remove any straight stems or they can take over the whole plant and you will lose the distinctive curly leaf shape.

3 Place the plant centrally in the new container. Back fill with more planting mixture. Make sure the container is completely filled and the plant is firmly seated in its new container.

4 Gently press down the planting mix so that no air pockets remain and the crown of the plant is level with the soil, which should be 1 in (2.5 cm) from the top of the pot.

5 Using a fine spray, thoroughly soak the mix. This will cause the soil level to fall slightly. Top with more planting mix so that the crown is at soil level again.

6 Finally, add a 1-in (2.5-cm) layer of aquarium gravel. Be sure to use gravel specifically sold for this purpose as some gravels contain pieces that will adversely affect water chemistry.

* When selecting marginals, be sure to consider the vigor of each type. Some can become invasive weeds if allowed to grow unchecked. For this reason, it is best to plant each species in its own planting basket rather than allow it a free root run.

7 Water the basket again. This watering needs to be very thorough and should take a few minutes to complete. You may need to top off the gravel if it has sunk in the container.

# Potting water lilies

There are huge numbers of species and varieties of water lily to choose from, but the cheapest and most commonly available are usually the very vigorous ones that grow far too large for the average garden pond. Always check out the planting depth and spread of a water lily before you buy it, and ideally select a named variety of the color and size you want. Bear in mind that one supplier's version of, say, a 'St. Louis Gold' may not be the same as another's.

*Water lilies grow from buds, or eyes, found on the rootstock, or rhizome.*

*The leaves are held on long thin stems. These are brittle and easily broken in transit.*

*The root system can be extensive and, in large varieties, may be too large for one person to lift.*

## POTTING A WATER LILY

1 Water lily rhizomes may be conical or horizontal (as here). Before planting, trim back any dead areas and check for signs of disease.

2 Place in a hole deep enough for the roots, with the growing tip pointing slightly upward and toward a corner. This type of lily grows along the basket until the tip is outside the container.

3 Lay the rest of the rhizome just level with the soil surface. Fill in the hole with aquatic potting mix and pat gently. Water well with a fine-spray watering can.

**4** The growing tip is still pointing upward and out of the mix. T should be level with the soil surface and the roots covered. Top with mix if necessary.

**5** Using a trowel, cover the soil surface with a 1-in (2.5-cm) layer of aquarium gravel. Other gravels may contain substances that are harmful to fish.

**6** Only the growing tip and a little of the rhizome are visible. After about three years, the growing tip will be hanging over the side, and the plant will need repotting.

## LARGER PLANTS FOR AN INSTANT DISPLAY

Many aquatic centers sell larger, more mature specimens of water lilies—often with flowers—in 2.5-gallon (10-liter) pots or larger. If you cannot wait a year or two for smaller ones to mature, these larger plants offer instant surface coverage and the bonus of flowers. The range of varieties available in larger sizes tends to be limited, so do not buy one if it is not the variety or size you want. Planting an unsuitable one may cause problems and disappointment later on if it grows too large or does not fit into the color scheme. If in any doubt, use a smaller one, and be patient while it matures.

▲ *Larger water lily specimens are tempting, but choose with care.*

# Deep water aquatics

Deep water aquatics have their roots growing in substrate and send up long stems to the water surface, where the leaves float. Strictly speaking, water lilies belong to this group, but it also includes some other excellent plants that should be grown more widely. They have the same requirements as water lilies, and when planted with lilies, they extend the flowering season and add interest to the pond. Their leaves—and often their flowers—are very attractive. Unlike water lilies, several of these plants will thrive in turbulent water. In addition, they do not need as much sunlight. They provide shade and refuge for fish and fish fry and a platform on which insects and amphibians can rest. Being hardy, they will survive moderately cold but not harsh winters.

◀ *The spatterdock (Nuphar lutea) is a hardy, vigorous plant that will succeed where water lilies fail, as it tolerates moving water and partial shade.*

*\* Cut back the stems of deep water aquatics such as Nymphoides peltata before planting.*

## PLANT CHOICES

*Aponogeton distachyos*—Water hawthorn
*Nuphar lutea*—Spatterdock
*Nymphoides peltata*—Water fringe
*Orontium aquaticum*—Golden club
For more details, see pages 86–87.

## PLANTING ADVICE

Deep water aquatics and water lilies are usually sold as container grown, and providing they do not look overgrown, you can place them directly into the pond. Remove any damaged leaves first.

## ADDING WATER LILIES

1 When you first put a water lily in its basket on the bottom of the pond, the leaves may not be able to float on the surface. You can use a clean, upturned plastic pot to raise up the lily to the correct height. A black pot will be less visible in the water.

2 To wash surplus soil from the basket, make sure that the lily is thoroughly watered before you place it in the pond. A generous layer of aquarium gravel spread over the soil surface prevents fish from digging out the soil and disturbing the plant as it becomes established.

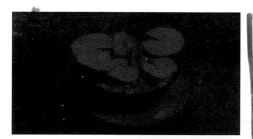

3 With the lily in the pond, the leaves should be about 1.5 in. (4 cm) below the water to allow them to grow to the surface. Depending on the temperature and variety, you will need to lower the lily every month until eventually the basket is resting on the bottom of the pond.

▶ If they are to thrive, all water lilies must have full, uninterrupted sunlight and little water movement.

# The bog garden

Normally, moisture-loving, or bog, plants are grown in planting baskets around the pond edge, but you can create a separate bed that will remain waterlogged year-round. To do this, dig out 18 in (45 cm) of soil and place some plastic sheeting or pond liner in its place. Puncture the bottom every 6 in (15 cm) with a garden fork, and make sure that the sheeting hangs over the edge of the excavation. Replace the original soil, and dig in several bags of well-rotted manure. Before planting, make sure the soil is thoroughly waterlogged. Always water this bed during prolonged dry spells.

## A BOG GARDEN

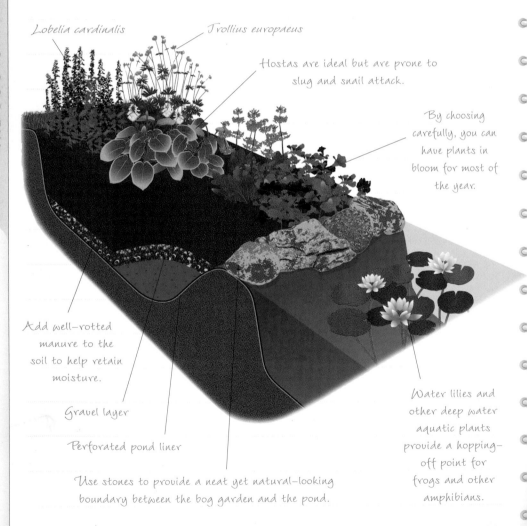

Lobelia cardinalis

Trollius europaeus

Hostas are ideal but are prone to slug and snail attack.

By choosing carefully, you can have plants in bloom for most of the year.

Add well-rotted manure to the soil to help retain moisture.

Gravel layer

Perforated pond liner

Use stones to provide a neat yet natural-looking boundary between the bog garden and the pond.

Water lilies and other deep water aquatic plants provide a hopping-off point for frogs and other amphibians.

1 Dig out the soil to a depth of 18 in (45 cm), and line the hole with pond liner. Using a garden fork, make drainage holes in the liner.

2 To prevent winter waterlogging, add a generous layer of up to 8 in (20 cm) of pea gravel. Rake it evenly over the base of the hole.

3 Add a length of irrigation hose. During dry periods, this can be connected to a tap for watering. Fill the excavation to the top with soil.

4 Add bare-rooted bog garden plants in spring. Pot-grown specimens can be planted all year round. Tease out congested roots.

*under red maple*

◀ Irises, hostas, sensitive fern, primulas, mimulus, lobelias, and astilbe add color and interest.

THE BOG GARDEN

# *Propagating plants*

Most aquatic plants are easy to propagate, whether by division or from seed, cuttings, eyes, or winter buds. Most floating plants reproduce asexually by sending out runners. These produce new plantlets every so often, which remain attached to the parent plant. Eventually, a whole carpet of plants will build up. You can propagate these plants easily throughout the growing season.

◀ The best tool for this job is a pair of strong, sharp scissors. If more than one plantlet is growing on the runner, separate each one carefully to produce several independent plants.

Water hyacinth
(*Eichhornia
crassipes*)

Trim the severed runner close to the mother plant.

▲ Water hyacinth produces runners fairly early on in the season. Separate the plantlets by cutting the runner close to the mother plant and again near the plantlet.

Divide plantlets from the mother plant only when they have a good root system.

◀ Water lettuce (Pistia stratiotes), *like many other floating plants, produces plantlets on runners. Once the plantlets reach a reasonable size, they can be separated from the parent plant.*

## FROGBIT AND WATER SOLDIER

As autumn approaches, the frogbit *(Hydrocharis morsus-ranae)* breaks up into several individual plantlets. At first, these are attached by runners, but eventually they turn into hard, fat, leafless buds that sink to the pond floor to overwinter. In a deep pond, it is going to take longer for the water to warm up and stir them into growth. To counter this, gather a few buds during the autumn, and overwinter them in a plastic bowl with a layer of soil on the bottom and filled with water. Place the bowl in a cool, frost-free but light position until early spring. The water soldier *(Stratiotes aloides)* behaves in a similar way but usually retains an old brittle plant around which are clustered tiny plantlets, each attached by a runner rather like the indoor spider plant. In due course, these either separate or can be divided and redistributed in spring.

◀ *Detach young plants of water soldier produced during the growing season.*

## PROPAGATING OXYGENATORS

Submerged aquatic plants (here *Lagarosiphon major*) can be increased by stem cuttings.

1 Make cuttings from new growth, ideally during spring.

2 Insert bunches of cuttings into a basket of aquatic potting mix.

3 Add a generous layer of well-washed pea gravel to prevent soil spillage.

4 Water the basket to expel air and place in the pond. The cuttings will grow rapidly.

PROPAGATING PLANTS

# Propagating plants (continued)

Marginal plants will need dividing every four to five years, or even sooner if they outgrow their welcome in the pond. For the majority of plants, division is simply a matter of splitting the crown or clump into sustainable portions and planting them individually. Always retain the youngest, most vigorous portions and discard the older material.

## DIVIDING IRIS PSEUDACORUS

Shorten the leaves with a sharp knife.

Break apart the young growths, leaving individual crowns with leaves and rootstock.

Plant the divisions singly into small mesh containers of aquatic mix. Water well and top off with gravel.

Reduce the length of the roots.

◀ When dividing irises, carefully lift the whole clump, ideally after flowering, so the divisions become established before the next flowering season.

▲ Position the basket on the marginal shelf, initially with water just lapping over the top. Once established, lower the basket.

PROPAGATING PLANTS

## DIVIDING CLUMP-FORMING MARGINALS

For most marginal plants, spring division is best, just as the new season's growth is appearing. Young plants then have the whole growing season before them.

1 Many marginals grow in tight clumps (this is *Mimulus ringens*). Propagate by lifting them periodically and separating them into individual plants. They establish quickly.

2 Cut back the foliage to within 2–4 in (5–10 cm) of the base and reduce the roots to 1 in (2–3 cm). Pot individually into small pots, and stand them in water just covering the rims.

## DIVIDING DWARF MARGINALS

▲ *Short-growing plants such as* Sisyrinchium angustifolium *produce many tiny divisions that can be treated like seedlings in a seed tray.*

▲ *Reduce the foliage and root growth of each division by about half. Plant in a seed tray filled with aquatic planting mixture.*

◀ *Let them stand in a tray of shallow water for about two months. Then pot each plant individually in aquatic potting mixture topped with pea gravel.*

# *Propagating plants (continued)*

A number of marginal aquatic plants, as well as most submerged plants and a sprinkling of bog garden subjects, can be increased by stem cuttings during spring and summer. These are short pieces of healthy, ideally nonflowering stem taken from recent growth.

▶ *Remove shoots up to 2 in (5 cm) long, cutting at a leaf joint. It is in this area that the cells that will be stimulated into producing roots will be most active. Remove the lower leaves to prevent them from decomposing in the water. Keep the cuttings moist as you prepare them.*

*\* There is no need to use a hormone rooting preparation when taking cuttings as most aquatic plants root very quickly.*

*Strip off flowers before using these shoots for cuttings.*

*Insert the cuttings in a pot of thoroughly soaked aquatic mix.*

*Place four cuttings around the edge of a 3 in (7.5 cm) plastic pot.*

*These are the ideal size for cuttings.*

▲ *Stand the pot in a bowl with water just covering the pot rim. After two to three weeks, separate the rooted cuttings into individual pots of aquatic potting mix. To encourage bushy growth, pinch out the growing tips.*

## WILL MY PLANT ROOT FROM A STEM CUTTING?

Generally speaking, if a plant has veins in a net arrangement (e.g., *Mimulus*), it can be increased from a stem cutting. If the leaves have parallel veins (e.g., *Iris*), then stem cuttings are not possible.

## DIVIDING A WATER LILY

A water lily with a conical rhizome, as here, can be divided if it has two or more growing points. Horizontal-growing rhizomes send out side shoots, which can be cut away to make separate plants.

1 Once you lift it from the pond, remove the water lily from its basket and wash off all the soil. This small plant with two distinct growing tips will easily divide into two plants.

2 Lay the plant on a firm, level surface, and using a sharp knife, cut the rhizome cleanly between the two growing points. In large plants the rhizome can be very tough to cut. Remove all superfluous foliage, and plant the crown firmly in a basket filled with aquatic potting mixture. Leave just the nose and any emerging leaves above soil level. Water the basket thoroughly, and cover it with a generous layer of pea gravel before placing it gently in the pond.

## WATER LILY PROPAGATION FROM EYES

1 Using a sharp knife, remove the eyes, plus a sliver of rootstock.

3 Place each pot in a bowl, covering the pot rim with water. As leaves develop, add more water.

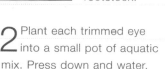

2 Plant each trimmed eye into a small pot of aquatic mix. Press down and water. Add a layer of pea gravel.

4 When the small pot is full of roots, the young water lilies are ready to be planted into the pond.

PROPAGATING PLANTS

# *Propagating plants (continued)*

Many deep water aquatic plants can be propagated by using the naturally produced runners as divisions. Simply cut them off and pot them up separately as shown below. Water fringe *(Nymphoides peltata)* is particularly easy to propagate in this way. Other deep water aquatics, such as golden club *(Orontium aquaticum)* and water hawthorn *(Aponogeton distachyos)*, can be raised from freshly collected seed. Planting seeds is an ideal way of increasing a variety of pond plants, including those in the bog garden.

## USING RUNNERS AS DIVISIONS

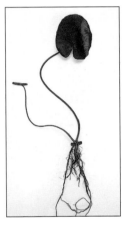

2 Select larger plantlets for repotting, ideally with several leaves (two, at the least) and a well-developed root system. Remove any damaged leaves.

1 Use sharp scissors to cut the runner on either side of the plantlet. Cut as close to the crown of the plantlet as possible without damaging it.

3 Partially fill a basket with aquatic potting mix, leaving a central hole for the root system. Lower the plant into position and backfill with mix. The crown should sit just level with the soil surface. Add a layer of aquarium gravel before placing the basket in the pond. This is water fringe *(Nymphoides peltata)*.

### COLLECTING SEEDS

The ripe seeds of many plants can be collected and sown into moist seed mix. Hosta seeds ripen on the lower parts of the flower stem first and are easy to germinate. They will probably not look identical to the parent plant, but you may produce a new form!

# RAISING AQUATIC PLANTS FROM SEED

1 Use a good-quality seed potting mixture, and distribute the seed sparingly over the surface of the seed tray.

2 Cover the seeds with a thin layer of mix, and press gently. Water the tray from above, and place it in standing water.

3 The water level in the outside tray should match the surface of the mix in the seed tray. Do not submerge seeds.

4 When the seedlings have germinated, plant them in a seed tray to grow. Handle the seedlings with care.

* True aquatic plants can often be raised from seed as long as it is freshly gathered, on the point of ripening, and sown immediately. Bog garden seeds are more conventional and some, such as mimulus and primula, are available commercially and can be sown in early spring.

5 Once the seed tray is full of roots, lift the young plants carefully and either pot them or plant them directly outside. These are *Mimulus* hybrids.

PROPAGATING PLANTS

# Color-themed planting

Many gardeners are attracted to the idea of a color-themed garden or area within the garden, and it is perfectly possible to introduce a color theme into your pond area. At its most dramatic, this can include the paving and other ornaments around the pond area. This idea works particularly well in a formal setting; for a more informal pond, confine the color theming to the planting scheme.

▶ *Pickerel weed (Pontederia cordata) has deep green, heart-shaped, glossy leaves. Blue-purple flower spikes appear in late summer and early autumn.*

▲ *There are many beautiful varieties of Siberian flag iris. This species does not require an acidic soil.*

◀ *'King of the Blues' is a tropical water lily that needs warmth and full sun to thrive in cool, temperate climates.*

## BLUE PLANTING SCHEME

*Eichhornia crassipes*
*Iris laevigata* 'Variegata'
*Iris sibirica* 'Ewen'
*Iris versicolor*
*Myosotis scorpioides*
*Pontederia cordata*
*Primula* Super giants series—blue
*Veronica beccabunga*

## TROPICAL WATER LILIES

No hardy water lilies are available with blue flowers, but you could use tropical varieties in summer and house them in frost-free conditions during the cold winter period.
Small    'Margaret May'
Medium 'Blue Beauty'
Large    *Nymphaea capensis*

## WHITE PLANTING SCHEME

*Alisma plantago-aquatica*
*Aponogeton distachyos*
*Astilbe* 'Irrlicht'
*Calla palustris*
*Caltha leptosepala*
*Hydrocharis morsus-ranae*
*Lysichiton camtschatcensis*
*Menyanthes trifoliata*
*Primula* 'Postford White'
*Sagittaria latifolia*
*Sagittaria sagittifolia* 'Flore Pleno'
*Saururus cernuus*
*Stratiotes aloides*
*Trapa natans*
*Zantedeschia aethiopica*

### WATER LILIES

Small   *Nymphaea odorata minor*
Medium 'Gonnère' and 'Virginalis'
Large   *Nymphaea alba*
          'Marliacea Albida'

▲ Sagittaria sagittifolia *'Flore Pleno'* is the fully double form of the common arrowhead. It tends to remain smaller and is considerably less invasive.

▶ Nymphaea *'Virginalis' is a medium-vigorous water lily suitable for medium-size ponds. Optimum planting depth is 16 in (40 cm).*

▲ Zantedeschia aethiopica *(arum lily)* reaches 12–36 in (30–90 cm). From early spring to early summer, the long stems are topped by white spathes 6–9 in (15–23 cm) long, with a bright yellow spadix.

*    When choosing white plants for a color-themed area, bear in mind that "white" can range from cold, pure shades to warm, almost creamy hues. Blend these colors carefully, and use them to link to other colors in adjoining areas.*

# Color-themed planting (continued)

Many of the early-flowering pond plants are yellow, particularly the marginals that come to life in the shallows as the days lengthen and the warmth of spring breathes life into the pond. Using pink and red flowers in and around the pond can complete a dazzling display that blends water plants with colorful garden subjects close by. Take account of the flowering periods of your plants to extend the interest as long as possible. Leaf shapes will also add variety to the scheme.

▲ Trollius europaeus *(globe flower) grows to 12–18 in (30–45 cm). This one has rich, golden yellow flowers on wiry stems. There are many varieties of this hardy plant; this is one of the earliest to flower.*

▲ Lysichiton americanus *(skunk cabbage) has deep golden yellow flowers borne on rubbery white stems in mid-spring. Very large, bright green leaves up to 36 in (90 cm) tall emerge after the flowers fade.*

▲ *'Texas Dawn' is a beautiful, large, bright yellow water lily. For a medium-size pond, try 'Sunrise', with its yellow, curved petals. For the small pond, 'Pygmaea Helvola' would be ideal.*

## YELLOW PLANTING SCHEME

*Caltha palustris*
*Caltha palustris* 'Flore Pleno'
*Carex elata* 'Bowles Golden'
*Cotula coronopifolia*
*Iris pseudacorus*
*Lysichiton americanus*
*Lysimachia nummularia*
*Mimulus luteus*
*Nuphar lutea*
*Nymphoides peltata*
*Orontium aquaticum*

*Primula elatior*
*Primula florindae*
*Ranunculus lingua*
*Trollius europaeus*

### WATER LILIES

Small    'Odorata Sulphurea'
       'Pygmaea Helvola'
Medium 'Sunrise'
Large    'Marliacea Chromatella'
       'Texas Dawn'

## RED AND PINK PLANTS

*Astilbe* x *arendsii* 'Bressingham Beauty'
*Astilbe* x *arendsii* 'Gertrud Brix'
*Astilbe* x *arendsii* 'Feuer'
*Astilbe chinensis* var. *pumila*
*Eupatorium purpureum*
*Hemerocallis* 'Pink Damask'
*Hemerocallis* 'Summer Wine'
*Iris ensata* 'Rose Queen'
*Lychnis* 'Rosea Plena'
*Lythrum salicaria* 'The Beacon'
*Lythrum salicaria* 'Robert'
*Primula vialii*
*Primula japonica*
*Primula secundiflora*
*Schizostylis coccinea* 'Grandiflora'

## WATER LILIES

Small    'Pygmaea Rubra'
Medium   'Froebelii'
           'James Brydon'
Large    'Escarboucle'

▲ Nymphaea *'James Brydon' has stunning pinkish crimson flowers. It is an old favorite for medium-size ponds but can become too vigorous in rich soil.*

*\* It is worth checking that everyone who uses the garden is happy with the choice of a color-themed pond before embarking on the planting.*

▼ *This pinky mauve day lily* (Hemerocallis) *is aptly named 'Summer Wine'.*

▲ *Astilbes are stunning bog garden plants that thrive in the damp soil close to the pond. There are many pink and red varieties to add dashes of color to poolside planting schemes.*

# *Spring plant care*

Ponds, and the life they contain, are very much at the mercy of the seasons. To keep them looking their best, they require regular care. As well as the tasks associated with the pond itself, such as cleaning filter media and checking pond equipment, the plants themselves will need attention. Spring is when a pond comes to life after a period of inactivity throughout winter. Now is the time to think about dividing water lilies and to add or replace bog and marginal plants.

## THE POND IN SPRING

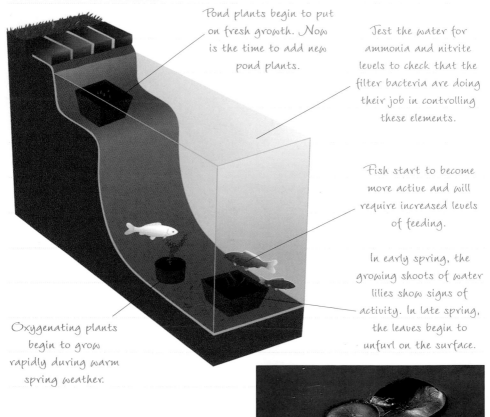

Pond plants begin to put on fresh growth. Now is the time to add new pond plants.

Test the water for ammonia and nitrite levels to check that the filter bacteria are doing their job in controlling these elements.

Fish start to become more active and will require increased levels of feeding.

In early spring, the growing shoots of water lilies show signs of activity. In late spring, the leaves begin to unfurl on the surface.

Oxygenating plants begin to grow rapidly during warm spring weather.

▶ As the water warms up in late spring, the leaves of water lilies slowly unfurl at the surface, and tadpoles make their appearance. If the pond has been netted for the winter, remove the net in time for frogs to gain access for spawning.

### ESSENTIAL TASKS

- Add new pond plants.
- Divide water lilies and marginal aquatics where necessary.
- Propagate water lilies from eyes.
- Take cuttings from submerged plants; replant where necessary.
- Sow seeds of commercially available bog garden and aquatic plants.
- Take stem cuttings of appropriate marginal aquatics.
- Repot and renew the potting mix of any appropriate plants that do not necessarily require dividing.

▲ *Test pond water for nitrite, nitrate, pH etc. using paper strip tests. Dip the strip into the water, wait one minute, and then compare colors with the chart provided.*

◀ *Long hours of sunlight, high levels of nitrates, and a lack of plant life in the pond can lead to a buildup of blanketweed (string, or hair, algae) and other algae in spring. Pond plants will soon starve out blanketweed, and you can remove the strands by hand (see page 43). Tackle green water with an ultraviolet light clarifier from early spring.*

▶ *A lovely display of bog primulas in spring provides color before the water lilies come into flower.*

# *Summer plant care*

Early summer is the time to divide many plants and add feed pellets to water lily containers. Cut back rampant growers, and deadhead plants that would spread seed far and wide. Lift baskets of submerged aquatic plants, and replace with cuttings. Renew half of your containers this way each year.

## THE POND IN SUMMER

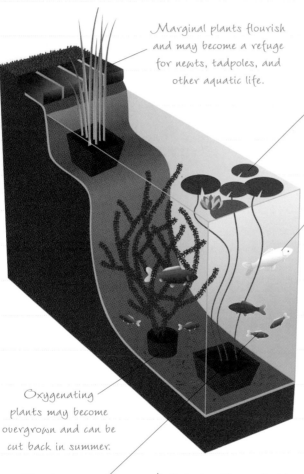

Marginal plants flourish and may become a refuge for newts, tadpoles, and other aquatic life.

The water lilies are in full flower. They add a splash of color and provide welcome shade at the surface of the pond.

Pond fish will be at their most active and may damage their scales after frantic spawning activity.

Oxygenating plants may become overgrown and can be cut back in summer.

Fish fry may be visible among the plants after summer spawning.

▶ *Select cutting material, ideally in late spring and midsummer, choosing fresh healthy stems with non-flowering lateral growth.*

## ESSENTIAL TASKS

- Control filamentous algae by twisting it out with a stick.
- Introduce new aquatic plants as required.
- Cut off faded blossoms of marginal plants, and remove any weeds.
- Net off surplus floating growth of carpeting plants, e.g., fairy moss.
- Take stem cuttings of appropriate marginal plants.
- Feed established water lilies and marginal plants.
- Sow freshly collected seeds of aquatic plants.
- Deadhead self-seeding plants, and cut back invasive species.
- Trim oxygenators to encourage new, more vigorous growth.

▼ *Before applying any chemical remedy against blanketweed (string algae), use a stick to remove large algal growths. This helps prevent water quality problems caused by blanketweed dying in the pond. Left unchecked, blanketweed clogs pond filters and tangles itself around oxygenating plants. Take care not to remove any fish or frogs.*

*\* Make time to enjoy the fruits of your labors! Summer is the time to relax by your flourishing pond.*

## SEPARATING PRIMULA PLANTLETS

Make divisions from the outer portions of plants, as these establish more quickly.

1 Lift bog garden plants such as primulas straight after flowering, and cut back the foliage greatly.

2 Separate plants and trim the roots back. Pot the small specimens. Plant the larger divisions directly outdoors.

# *Autumn plant care*

Once the first frosts hit in temperate zones, all the herbaceous plants will need trimming back. Any that need winter protection should be covered with fleece or straw to protect their crowns. Where weather is severe, remove oxygenating plants.

## THE POND IN AUTUMN

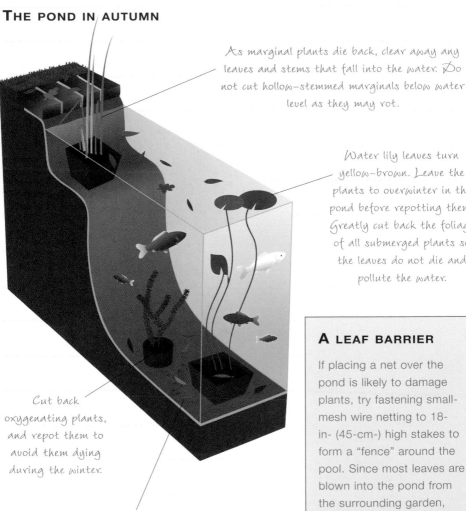

As marginal plants die back, clear away any leaves and stems that fall into the water. Do not cut hollow-stemmed marginals below water level as they may rot.

Water lily leaves turn yellow-brown. Leave the plants to overwinter in the pond before repotting them. Greatly cut back the foliage of all submerged plants so the leaves do not die and pollute the water.

Cut back oxygenating plants, and repot them to avoid them dying during the winter.

Cover the pond with a net to prevent water quality problems caused by decaying plant matter.

## A LEAF BARRIER

If placing a net over the pond is likely to damage plants, try fastening small-mesh wire netting to 18-in- (45-cm-) high stakes to form a "fence" around the pool. Since most leaves are blown into the pond from the surrounding garden, rather than falling directly from trees, the netting acts as a barrier against which they can collect.

## ESSENTIAL TASKS

- Collect and store plantlets and corms of appropriate aquatics ready for winter.
- Net the pond to keep out leaves.
- Cut back all faded aquatic plants, including reeds and many grasses.
- Take root cuttings of bog garden plants, such as primulas.

▲ *Here is a pond margin in late fall with the usual mix of fallen leaves and broken stems. Keep the water as clear as possible.*

## TAKING ROOT CUTTINGS

1 Lift a suitable plant and remove some fleshy roots, about a quarter-inch (5 mm) thick. Replant the parent in its original spot; it should reestablish quickly.

2 Cut roots into pieces three-quarters of an inch (2 cm) in length. Discard thin stringy portions. Keep the cuttings moist and plant them immediately.

3 Space out the cuttings evenly on the surface of multipurpose potting mixture in a seed tray.

4 Cover with mix, press down, and water. Store in a cold frame; root cuttings do not respond well if kept warm.

# Winter plant care

Winter is the time to check that slightly tender plants wrapped in fleece or straw still have their protective cover in place, particularly after a storm. Winter is also the ideal opportunity to take stock and plan ahead. Time spent looking through new plant catalogs is time well spent.

## THE POND IN WINTER

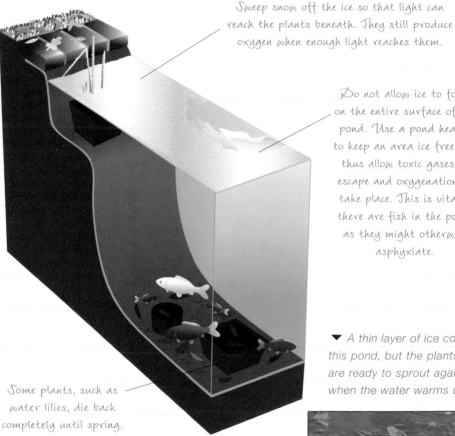

Sweep snow off the ice so that light can reach the plants beneath. They still produce oxygen when enough light reaches them.

Do not allow ice to form on the entire surface of the pond. Use a pond heater to keep an area ice free and thus allow toxic gases to escape and oxygenation to take place. This is vital if there are fish in the pond, as they might otherwise asphyxiate.

Some plants, such as water lilies, die back completely until spring.

▼ A thin layer of ice covers this pond, but the plants are ready to sprout again when the water warms up.

* Cover tender plants, such as gunnera, with old leaves, straw, or fleece to protect them from the frost.

## STORING PLANTS OVER WINTER

Most floating plant species produce winter buds, or corms, which will start to grow much earlier in the spring if given some winter protection.

1 Water hyacinth *(Eichhornia crassipes)* is not frost hardy. Detach young, vigorous plantlets, and overwinter them indoors in cool temperate climates.

2 Place the plantlets in a shallow bowl filled with a generous layer of aquatic potting mixture. Keep in full light at 50°F (10°C).

1 To overwinter water lettuce *(Pistia stratiotes)*, select vigorous young plantlets still attached to the parent.

2 Separate the plantlets. Put them in a bowl of water with soil at the bottom. Keep in strong light at 64°F (18°C).

▶ *Ceratophyllum demersum, or hornwort, produces small, brushlike winter buds. Place a few of these in a jar of water with soil at the bottom, and keep the container in the light to encourage some early growth.*

WINTER PLANT CARE

# *Pests and diseases*

As with all other plants, those grown in and around the pond are subject to attack by pests and diseases. Fortunately, few of these are particularly damaging to the plant and most can be controlled by good management of the environment. Bear in mind that fish and wildlife that live in and around the pond are adversely affected by chemicals used to control serious pests and outbreaks of disease. If any chemical treatments are to be used, a separate quarantine pond or holding area for creatures will be essential.

## AQUATIC SNAILS

Above or below the water surface, snails eat plants. The best defense is not to introduce them in the first place. Check all new plants for snails, no matter how small, and investigate all leaf and stem surfaces for lumps of clear jelly with little black spots in it. These are snail eggs. Picking snails out by hand is the only reliable control. Try floating a fresh lettuce leaf on the water overnight and discarding the snails that congregate beneath it the following morning.

◀ *Snail eggs in a blob of jelly are easy to miss.*

▲ *The greater pond snail will feed on algae but much prefers to graze on aquatic plants.*

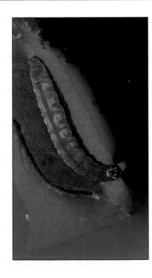

*\* Even if pond plants are your principal interest, it is a good idea to introduce a few fish to the pond to control mosquito larvae and aquatic insect pests. Common goldfish are cheap, tough, and reliable.*

◀ *In late summer, the china mark moth lays its eggs on floating-leaved plants. These hatch into caterpillars that live in "bivouacs" made from spinning together two cut pieces of leaf. After hibernating, they return in spring, shredding leaves and causing extensive damage. Remove any caterpillars you find, cut back surface foliage in extreme cases, and net out floating debris that may have larvae attached.*

## CADDIS FLY LARVAE

Caddis fly larvae feed on aquatic plants and create silky cases covered in bits of stick, sand, plant leaf, etc. They are minor pest in ponds, and a good fish population will keep them under control.

▶ *Iris sawfly larvae feed on the leaf surface of flag irises. Remove any caterpillars you find. Damage occurs in early summer and in autumn, when the sawfly breeds.*

◀ *Most gardeners welcome dragonflies to the pool, although fish lovers are not enthusiastic about them laying eggs in waterside vegetation, as these turn into voracious larvae that prey on small fish.*

*\* Water lily beetle larvae chew a furrow across the top of the water lily leaf. The surrounding tissue dies off, and eventually the whole leaf decays. In summer, knock the creatures into the pool with a strong jet of water so the fish can devour them.*

## WATER LILY APHIDS

These pests breed rapidly during warm humid weather, attacking the flowers and foliage of water lilies and other succulent aquatics. In winter, wash nearby cherry and plum trees to destroy overwintering populations. In summer, hose aphids into the pond with a strong jet of water. Do not use insecticides in a pond containing fish.

▶ *Water lily aphids spoil the beauty of the flowers.*

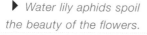

# *Pests and diseases (continued)*

Fortunately, there are few diseases that attack aquatic plants, and with the exception of water lily crown rot. they are fairly innocuous. The two common forms of water lily leaf spot are disfiguring but rarely cause the plant to die.

## MILDEW

Occasionally, marginal aquatics, especially marsh marigolds (*Caltha* sp.), suffer from mildew. This grayish mold attacks the foliage, usually long after flowering. It is ugly rather than debilitating and usually associated with poor growing conditions. For example, they may be planted too deep in the water or kept too dry. Mostly, the best way to deal with mildew is to cut off the infected foliage. In severe cases, move the plant in its container well away from the pond, and spray it with a systemic fungicide. Do not return the plant to the pond until the chemical has had time to dry on the foliage.

▲ *The beauty of the marsh marigold's foliage in early spring is sometimes spoiled by mildew as autumn approaches. Remove infected foliage.*

*\* Systemic fungicides work by being absorbed through the foliage of the plant and circulating through the sap stream, effectively inoculating the plant against attack. Such treatment will often be necessary a second time.*

▲ *Fish eat all kinds of insects that can become a nuisance, especially mosquito larvae. Fish will thrive in clean ponds.*

## WATER LILY LEAF SPOT

There are two forms of this disease. In one, reddish brown spots appear on both the upper and lower surface of the water lily pads. These enlarge and the center rots away. The only solution is to remove all affected leaves before they have a chance to pass on the infection. The other form starts along the edge of the leaves, causing them to turn brown and crumble. There is no set pattern for attack; in some years the problem is persistent, while in others it does not appear at all. This seems to be related to the weather conditions, especially temperature. Water lilies do best in full sunlight.

## WATER LILY CROWN ROT

This disease can be devastating. The water lily rhizome starts to turn black, and the leaves turn yellow and fall off. There is no cure, so check all new water lily rhizomes for any sign of a soft, black, foul-smelling area. If you even suspect the disease, do not introduce the plant to your pond. It is infectious and will spread to other lilies in the pond. If it should take hold, remove and destroy affected crowns, remove the fish, and clean out the pond thoroughly. Fill a muslin bag with copper sulphate crystals and swirl it vigorously through the water as a disinfection before final draining. Then reintroduce fresh clean water, and replant the pond.

▲ *If you suspect disease in a water lily, cut through the rhizome, and check for brown discoloration caused by crown rot.*

◀ *It may become necessary to clean out the pond, perhaps because plants have taken over to such an extent that the water is barely visible. The best time to do this is in early spring or late autumn after the first frosts, which kill off any foliage.*

# Popular Pond Plants

A well-planted, well-balanced pond is usually aesthetically pleasing because it embraces all classes of pond plant in moderate quantities with sufficient open water to add to their appeal. Then, by selecting specific plants within each category, you can begin to paint a horticultural picture. Most aquatic plants are simple to grow and offer great diversity. In order to produce an attractive and easily maintained water garden feature, it is essential to learn something about their "behavior" before introducing plants to the pond. In addition to creating a floral picture, plants make a major contribution to wildlife, whether this is intended or not. Many native and introduced aquatic plants, especially among the marginals, have an important role to play in the life cycle of butterflies and other insects. Beneath the water, the trailing roots of floating plants and the fine, fernlike, congested foliage of submerged aquatics provide living quarters for aquatic insect life and a haven for spawning fish and emerging fry.

Pond plants are the mainstay of a water feature, and in addition to all their practical benefits and aesthetic values, they have an individual fascination. No other part of the plant kingdom offers such a rich diversity of habit, character, and color.

The selection of pond plants offered for sale has increased dramatically, and it is now possible to create a pond full of color and interest year-round. Whether you are experimenting with color themes

Sepals · Stamens · Petals · Ovary · Peduncle

▶ Nymphaea *'Attraction' is a typical hardy water lily with colorful flowers to attract pollinating insects.*

Stigma—female part

Stamens—male parts

Outer petal

Peduncle

Ovary, where seeds will form

Sepal

◀ *Although it appears to be a very complex flower, a cross section shows it to be a typical inflorescence. All the familiar components are clear to see.*

Median petal

Outer petal

Sepal

▶ *Water lily flowers are usually seen from above, a view that reveals their symmetrical beauty. The blossoms float until fertilized, after which they slowly submerge.*

Inner petal

Stamen

Stigma

or a particular style of pond (say, a wildlife pond), you will need specific plants to create the desired effect. Whatever type of effect you are trying to create, read up as much as you can before buying any plants, as some can grow very large and be unsuitable for smaller ponds and gardens. This part of the book features a selection of pond plants, from oxygenators and floating plants to marginals, water lilies, and other deep water aquatic species. There is also an overview of suitable bog plants.

# *Oxygenating plants*

...ierged plants are the unsung heroes of the water garden. Most are fairly modest foliage plants with poor or insignificant flowers, but do not be misled. As well as providing oxygen for pond life, they play a vital role in utilizing the nutrients otherwise exploited by water-discoloring algae.

▼ *Hornwort* (Ceratophyllum demersum) *tends to grow as a free-floating mass of branching stems. Pieces that break away grow into individual plants.*

▲ *The small, bright green leaves of starwort* (Callitriche verna) *have a cresslike appearance. This evergreen plant will thrive in full sun in a mature pond. Very small flowers appear in late summer.*

▶ *Hairgrass* (Eleocharis acicularis) *spreads by runners, forming a dense "lawn." Depending on conditions, it can grow 2–10 in (5–25 cm) tall.*

\* Oxygenating plants are also described as hardy submerged plants. Most do best in water 18—36 in (45—90 cm) deep.

Elodea canadensis is sometimes sold as Egeria densa, which it resembles.

Small, dark-green leaves are arranged in dense whorls along extensive branching stems.

▼ Willow moss (Fontinalis antipyretica) *is an evergreen that continues to act as an oxygenator, even in winter.*

Fish enjoy eating the younger shoots.

▲ Canadian pondweed (Elodea canadensis) *is an attractive but very vigorous plant. It is easy to control when grown in a basket but will smother any pond with a mud or soil substrate.*

# Oxygenating plants (continued)

Without oxygenating and floating plants, the only way to maintain water clarity is with a pond filter, and there are a number of types of filters on the market. Oxygenating and floating plants, however, are both aesthetically pleasing and offer places for pondlife to hide, feed, and reproduce.

Curved, green leaves are set in whorls. Young foliage is paler green in color.

▲ *Water violet (Hottonia palustris) produces spikes of off-white or lilac blossoms above submerged foliage. It spreads slowly to form a clump, but later in the season stems break away.*

◀ *Fish weed (Lagarosiphon major, or Elodea crispa) thrives in full sun or partial shade. Grow it in baskets, and cut it back by two-thirds in autumn.*

▲ *Spiked milfoil (Myriophyllum spicatum) has long trailing stems and fine, feathery, reddish green submerged foliage. It produces red flowers held about 1 in (2.5 cm) above the water surface.*

◄ *Curled pondweed (Potamo__
crispus) is not often offered f___
is an excellent oxygenator an___
become invasive. Green strap____ ____
turn bronze or even red in full sun.*

▲ *Whorled water milfoil (Myriophyllum
verticillatum) has light green, needlelike
foliage. It is a submerged plant that does
well in the shallower areas of ponds.*

◄ ▼ *Water crowfoot (Ranunculus
aquatilis) has submerged, threadlike
foliage (shown at left), plus round floating
leaves and a profusion of white and yellow
flowers in late spring (shown below).*

## *Floating plants*

Apart from their decorative merit, free-floating hardy aquatic plants serve a practical role in creating an ecological balance. They reduce the light levels beneath the water and make life intolerable for single-celled and filamentous algae.

▶ *Water hyacinth (Eichhornia crassipes) has dark green, waxy leaves with swollen air-filled stems and large hyacinth-blue flowers in late summer.*

◀ *Frogbit (Hydrocharis morsus-ranae) resembles a miniature water lily. This is considered an invasive plant in the United States.*

▼ ▶ *Floating fern (Salvinia sp.) has a horizontal main shoot, with leaves above the water and clumps of roots below.*

◀ *Water chestnut* (Trapa natans) *has rosettes of glossy, dark green leaves with small, white flowers in summer. Nuts only appear after prolonged spells of warm summer sunshine.*

In cool climates, replace the plant every year.

▼ *Water soldier* (Stratiotes aloides) *is a free-floating plant with no fixed root system. From above, it closely resembles the top of a pineapple floating on the water.*

## INVASIVE FLOATING PLANTS

Floating plants draw their nutrients from the pond water, using a mass of fine trailing roots. They can grow and multiply without having to push through the soil, so they can spread rapidly. The beautiful water hyacinth *(Eichhornia crassipes)* has become a pest species in some southern parts of the United States, where it thrives in the warm climate. It is a native of South America and Australia, as well as Africa, where it is grazed by hippos. In cool temperate climates, it is treated as an annual plant or overwintered indoors, as it cannot survive winter.

▼ *In a sunny position sheltered from chill winds, water lettuce* (Pistia stratiotes) *grows to a height of 6 in (15 cm).*

FLOATING PLANTS

# Marginal plants

Marginal plants enjoy growing in the shallow waters at the pondside. Although they have little impact on the ecological balance of the pond, they provide much of the color, variety, and decorative interest from spring until the autumn.

*The seedhead resembles an elongated pine cone.*

▲ *The bright green, oval-leaved water plantain* (Alisma plantago-aquatica) *has long-lasting, pyramidal flower spikes that can grow more than 24 in (60 cm) tall.*

▲ *The variegated sweet flag* (Acorus calamus 'Variegatus') *is grown for its beautiful swordlike foliage. In spring, the vertically striped green and cream leaves are flushed rose pink toward their bases.*

◀ *The brilliant white spathes of bog arum* (Calla palustris) *are produced in spring, followed by orange or red fruits on female plants.*

*\* To propagate bog arum, sow the ripe seeds onto saturated soil. Alternatively, cut the rambling stems into sections, each with a healthy bud, and plant in saturated soil in late spring.*

## INCREASING BUTOMUS

1 Lift the p... wash the rootstock to expose the corms.

2 Remove the tiny corms, leaving each with a vestige of root attached.

▲ *Flowering rush* (Butomus umbellatus) *has rich green leaves that can grow 35 in (90 cm). The clusters of pink flowers are even taller, although it can be some time before the plant is mature enough to flower.*

▼ *Marsh marigold* (Caltha palustris) *has buttercup yellow flowers on stems up to 18 in (45 cm) long, held above a mound of glossy, green leaves. Excellent in early spring.*

3 Trim the roots, and place three or four corms in aquatic potting mix. Stand the pot in a bowl of tapwater just covering the rim. Grow until the corms are large enough to pot individually.

▶ *A compact plant for small ponds,* Caltha palustris *'Flore Pleno' produces double flowers in spring and again in autumn.*

▶ *Caltha palustris var.* alba *bears white flowers with yellow centers.*

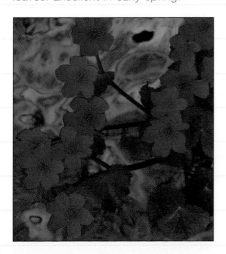

# *Marginal plants (continued)*

When arranging plants in an informal water feature, especially marginal and bog garden subjects, take account of flowering periods and any opportunities for creating pleasing contrasts and combinations of character and color. Cotton grass *(Eriophorum angustifolium)* and water forget-me-not *(Myosotis scorpioides)* always combine happily.

## THE UMBRELLA PLANT

The umbrella plant *(Cyperus alternifolius)* is well named, as its spiky leaves radiate from the stems like an umbrella. It is one of the most versatile marginal plants, as it will grow well in both temperate and tropical climates. However, it will not overwinter outdoors where there is a danger of frost. In such circumstances, it can spend the winter indoors as a pot plant.

▲ *The aptly named brass buttons* (Cotula coronopifolia) *has small, bright yellow flowers. The fine foliage makes a lush mat in spring but may deteriorate once the flowers are over. However, new growth will soon appear after a quick trim.*

▲ Carex pendula *droops gracefully over the water from the marginal shelf. It forms tall clumps that are resistant to waterfowl.*

▲ *Cotton grass* (Eriophorum angustifolium) *needs acid conditions to thrive, so mix plenty of peat into a rich soil. It prefers a position in full sun and is not as invasive as many other grasslike plants.*

▲ *Both the stems and roots of* Cyperus longus *are sweetly scented, hence the plant's common name, sweet galingale. Plant this tough, invasive plant in a container to keep it under control.*

▶ *In spring, variegated water grass* (Glyceria maxima *var.* variegata) *has cream-striped leaves flushed pink at the base.*

◀ Houttuynia cordata *'Chameleon' is a stunning ground cover but can become invasive and will need cutting back.*

▶ Equisetum hyemale *is a horsetail with black bands up the stems.*

MARGINAL PLANTS

# *Marginal plants (continued)*

Irises are wonderful plants in all settings, their bold architectural fans of leaves creating valuable contrasts to the shapes of other plants, such as marsh marigolds and bogbean (buckbean). Of all the marginal plants, it is the irises that show the richest diversity. They are of varying stature and have flowers of almost every color and combination

imaginable. Although principally grown for their beautiful blossoms, their swordlike foliage can be magnificent, particularly that of the variegated varieties, and they produce quite dramatic architectural effects, especially in the formal pond.

◀ *Plant Asiatic water lilies* (Iris laevigata) *in large groups in full sun and waterlogged soil, with just 1–2 in (2.5–5 cm) of water above the rhizome.*

## VARIETIES OF IRIS LAEVIGATA

*Iris laevigata* has sired many very fine aquatic varieties in a range of colors to suit every type of pond planting.

'Albopurpurea'—purple and white
'Atropurpurea'—reddish purple
'Colchesterensis'—white and dark blue
'Lilacina'—light blue
'Midnight'—deep blue, lined white
'Mottled Beauty'—white mottled with
    pale blue
'Rose Queen'—soft rose pink
'Snowdrift'—double-flowered white

▲ Iris *'Colchesterensis', a favorite variety of* I. laevigata, *has gorgeous six-petalled flowers in rich purple and white.*

*In* Iris laevigata *'Variegata' the cream and green colors are well separated. Late summer blue flowers are short lived; when mature, the group offers a good flowering period.*

▶ *The yellow flag (Iris pseudacorus) grows rather large for the average pond. There are variegated forms that are less vigorous.*

▼ Iris laevigata *'Midnight' is a stunning dark blue, with contrasting tongues of white on the graceful petals.*

▶ *Blue flag (Iris versicolor) has bluish green, stiffly held leaves. The flowers are blue with a hint of violet. The variety 'Kermesina' (right) has wine-red flowers marked with yellow.*

# *Marginal plants (continued)*

...allow you to grow plants with a water depth requirement ranging from ...in (30 cm) of water. Always refer to plant labels for information about the ideal planting depth when buying new species or varieties of marginals.

Remove any straight foliage that may appear. Greenish brown flower clusters are produced during midsummer.

◀ *The corkscrew rush* Juncus effusus *'Spiralis' produces spirals of green, cylindrical leaves growing in all directions.*

▼ *The yellow skunk cabbage* (Lysichiton americanus) *has arumlike spathes in very early spring, followed by large leaves that make good cover along pond margins.*

\* *Lysichiton camtschatcensis from Asia is not as large as L. americanus, which can grow to 24—36 in (60—90 cm). Once mature, the immense foliage of L. camtschatcensis is just part of the effect, forming the backdrop to the enormous white arum spathe and central flower spike.*

◀ *Water mint* (Mentha aquatica) *has scented leaves and pretty purple flowers that attract insects all through the summer.*

▲ *Bogbean* (Menyanthes trifoliata) *contrasts with upright-growing marginals as it scrambles across the ground and water surface.*

▼ Mimulus guttatus *(yellow musk) has yellow flowers, occasionally spotted with red. This plant does best in waterlogged soil.*

## MONKEY MUSK

*Mimulus*, or monkey musk, is one of the earliest plants to flower and, if deadheaded, can flower all summer and into the autumn. If allowed to set seed, it soon appears everywhere. The best hardy variety is *M. luteus*. Its large yellow flowers with dark red spots over mid-green leaves brighten even the darkest corner. Many hybrids are available: 'Queen's Prize' has

bigger, brighter flowers than *M. luteus,* and its more compact habit makes it suitable for the smaller pond.

*Remove flowers as they finish, and cut down stems to encourage growth.*

# Marginal plants (continued)

As well as offering height and shade around the pond, marginals allow wildlife access to and from the pond. Their range of shapes and colors increases the overall visual effect that you can create in and around the pond.

◀ *Water forget-me-not* (Myosotis scorpioides) *has small, pale blue flowers held close to the water surface.*

◀ Phalaris arundinacea *is a graceful grass but has an invasive habit. The striped variety 'Picta' shown here is a safer and more elegant choice.*

## WATER CRESS

Water cress *(Nasturtium officinale)* is a very useful plant in the pond. Used correctly it can reduce algae growth. Because it grows so quickly, it uses up any excess nutrients in the water and starves the algae. Crop it regularly to encourage new growth. Plant it in baskets without soil so that the plant has to extract the nutrients from the water rather than from the soil.

▲ *Cut off the flowers of water cress as they finish; otherwise, they set seed and the plant will die off.*

▶ Oenanthe javanica *'Flamingo' is grown for its fernlike foliage of grey-green leaves tipped with pink and cream. It can be invasive if it escapes to the garden, but in the pond it creates a colorful display all year.*

▼ *Pickerel weed* (Pontederia cordata) *takes a season to become established, but then produces delightful bright, glossy green, heart-shaped foliage and spikes of soft blue flowers in late summer.*

# *Marginal plants (continued)*

When planting a pond, consider the aspect for viewing, and arrange the taller varieties of marginals along the far bank and sides of the pond, with the lower-growing plants along the front bank. If there is a filter or pump housing to hide, use tall, bushy plants to mask them. Check the plant labels at aquatic dealers for information on mature plant heights.

◀ *Greater spearwort (Ranunculus lingua 'Grandiflora') has dark green foliage and bright yellow, saucerlike flowers during midsummer.*

▼ *Lizard tail (Saururus cernuus) has tiny, white, fragrant flowers and olive green, heart-shaped leaves that are brighter on the underside. It is one of the few marginals with autumn color; its leaves turn bright crimson.*

▼ *Water buttercup (Ranunculus lingua) is a tall-growing relative of the terrestrial buttercup. Plant it in a large basket in a rich, loamy soil.*

Pretty yellow flowers are held above the plant on wiry stems.

During the summer, mature plants send up flower spikes of single white flowers with greenish or yellow centers.

The common arrowhead prefers full sun and water at least 6 in (15 cm) deep. Divide overgrown clumps in spring or summer.

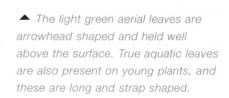

▲ The light green aerial leaves are arrowhead shaped and held well above the surface. True aquatic leaves are also present on young plants, and these are long and strap shaped.

◀ The glossy mid-green leaves of Sagittaria sagittifolia 'Flore Pleno' offset the triangular stems of double white flowers. Provide rich, acidic soil in shallow water.

MARGINAL PLANTS

# Marginal plants (continued)

...ifferent marginal plants provides the varied habitat needed by pond ...phibians. Emerging dragonflies climb out onto tall rushes and irises to dry their wings; spawning frogs favor low-growing "rafting" plants, such as brooklime, forget-me-not, and water cress, which spread out from their baskets in floating mats.

## REEDS AND RUSHES: PROBLEM VARIETIES

Avoid all species of plain green *Juncus*, *Carex,* and the smaller *Schoenoplectus*. These are weedy species that seed themselves freely and can swamp a pond. A number, such as *Juncus effusus* and *Carex riparia*, are offered for sale for wildlife ponds, but they can become really pernicious and create serious maintenance problems.

▲ Schoenoplectus lacustris *'Albescens'* *is a tall, vertically striped rush. Cut it back in winter to about 6 in (15 cm), and retrim in spring to encourage new shoots.*

▶ *With its horizontally banded stems,* Schoenoplectus lacustris *'Zebrinus' makes an interesting addition to the garden pond.*

◀ *Narrow-leaved reedmace,* Typha angustifolia, *is suitable only for a larger or wildlife pond. The fruiting heads are often used for dried indoor decoration.*

▲ *The trailing stems of brooklime* (Veronica beccabunga) *are ideal for disguising the pool edge. Dark blue flowers appear above dark green foliage.*

▼ Typha minima *is ideal for the small pond, but grow it in a pot as its hardiness means it will outgrow weaker plants.*

▲ *Arum lily* (Zantedeschia aethiopica) *is one of the easiest water plants to grow.*

MARGINAL PLANTS

# *Pygmy water lilies*

Pygmy water lilies are complete miniature replicas of standard varieties. They have the same flowering season, which extends from early summer until autumn. They can be grown in tubs, sinks, and containers and in the larger pond as well, providing the depth is suitable. True pygmy kinds often occupy positions on the marginal shelves.

▲ Nymphaea x pygmaea *'Alba' is a perfect miniature water lily for growing in a container or in the pond margins.*

## OVERWINTERING PYGMY WATERLILIES

While most water lilies require constant immersion in water to thrive, the pygmy kinds can be removed and stored in damp conditions for the winter. Drain the water from the tub in which the water lilies are growing, and keep the plants damp in their potting mixture until spring. Once water is added again, the plants will grow away strongly.

◄ N. *'Pygmaea Helvola' produces bright yellow flowers above brown-speckled leaves all summer long. The maximum spread is 18 in (45 cm).*

◀ *Nymphaea odorata minor is the smallest of the white lilies and ideal for tubs and small patio ponds. The flowers are sweetly scented and surrounded by small green leaves.*

▼ *N. 'Pygmaea Rubra' is easy to grow and quite hardy for a small lily. It may be offered for sale by other names; either buy a flowering plant or seek out a specialist nursery.*

## CULTIVATION

All water lilies need full, uninterrupted sunlight if they are to prosper. With pygmy and small-growing varieties, it is important to top the pool or container regularly with water to replace that lost by evaporation. Neglecting to do this will result in a rapid deterioration of the plants. These otherwise easy going plants require repotting and replanting every three years and fertilizing regularly during the seasons between. Propagation is by division or eyes and, in the case of *Nymphaea* 'Pygmaea Alba', seed as well.

PYGMY WATER LILIES

# Small water lilies

Small water lilies have a maximum spread of 24 in (60 cm) and need only be planted 4–10 in (10–25 cm) deep. They are ideal for smaller ponds and provide maximum surface cover of about 1 ft$^2$ (0.3 m²)· The leaf size varies from 1–2 in (2.5–5 cm), and the flowers are 2–4 in (5–10 cm) across, depending on the variety.

▲ N. 'Hermine' has tulip-shaped blossoms of the purest white, held above dark green oval foliage.

▲ Throughout the summer, N. 'Graziella' freely produces orange-red flowers, scarcely more than 2 in (5 cm) in diameter, and with deep orange stamens.

▶ Of the small pinks, N. 'Laydekeri Lilacea', with a spread of 24 in (60 cm), is one of the best. Pale pink, scented blooms darken with age. The leaves have with reddish brown spots.

## PLANTING SMALL WATER LILIES

Plant small water lilies in a 1 gallon (3- or 4-liter) pot. When you first put the container in the pond, raise it up on some stones so that the crown of the plant is only 4 in (10 cm) below the water surface. As new leaves grow up to the surface, lower the water lily basket a little each week until it is at its final planting depth.

◀ Nymphaea *'Laydekeri Purpurata'* has crimson red flowers with bright orange stamens held above maroon-flecked leaves that are purple underneath.

▼ N. *'William Falconer'* produces blood red flowers with bright yellow stamens. In its early stages of growth, the foliage has a distinctive purplish hue.

▲ The scented flowers of N. *'Odorata Sulphurea'* are held above the water.

SMALL WATER LILIES

# Medium-size water lilies

Medium-size water lilies range in size up to plants with a maximum spread of 60 in (150 cm). They require a planting depth of between 6 and 24 in (15 and 60 cm), although most seem to do best at 18 in (45 cm). They produce blooms measuring 4–7 in (10–18 cm) across and are available in a wide range of colors. All the medium-size water lilies popularly offered for sale are completely winter hardy in cool temperate climates.

▲ N. 'Marliacea Albida' is a free-flowering scented lily with clear white blooms and conspicuous golden yellow stamens.

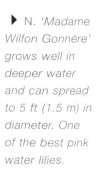

▲ Nymphaea 'Froebelii' is an old, very hardy variety. Once well established, it flowers freely from late spring into early autumn.

▶ N. 'Madame Wilfon Gonnère' grows well in deeper water and can spread to 5 ft (1.5 m) in diameter. One of the best pink water lilies.

## HISTORY

The medium-size water lilies include many varieties originally produced by the legendary French water lily breeder M. Joseph Bory Latour-Marliac. The first of these appeared in 1877 and was followed by an incredible number of varieties developed over a thirty-year period. Sadly, his secret methods died with him in 1911, and it has only been in recent years that other breeders have started to discover this lost art.

▲ N. 'Gonnère' is a truly stunning plant, with large, white double flowers over green leaves. Ideal for medium-size ponds.

▼ N. 'James Brydon' can be too vigorous, but planting it in poorer soil can encourage flowering and may help to slow down leaf production.

MEDIUM-SIZE WATER LILIES

# Medium-size water lilies (continued)

Among this group of water lilies, flower shapes vary from starlike in 'Rose Arey' to peony shaped in 'James Brydon' and cup shaped in 'Marliacea Albida'. Unlike the tropical varieties, which raise their flowers above the water, most of the hardy kinds float on the water surface among the water lily pads.

MEDIUM-SIZE WATER LILIES

◀ *The flowers of N. odorata rosea grow up to 5 in (13 cm) across. It can adapt to a planting depth of 10–24 in (25–60 cm) and will spread to 60 in (150 cm).*

▼ *Nymphaea 'Mrs Richmond' is a very popular water lily. The flowers are cup shaped and freely produced.*

▶ *N. 'Marliacea Chromatella' has beautiful, slightly scented flowers and fine, boldly marked foliage.*

◀ *N. 'Moorei' is a free-flowering, soft yellow variety, ideal for the medium-size pond.*

## VARIABLE WATER LILIES

Most lilies in the variable group have yellow to orange flowers that gradually change to deep orange or red. They are suitable for warmer positions in the pond and thrive in shallow water. They are prolific bloomers, and their changing colors add to their value in the pond.

▶ *The new flowers of Nymphaea 'Sioux' open to a bright apricot and deepen to red-orange with age. Suitable for medium to large ponds.*

◀ *Nymphaea odorata 'Alba' is a very hardy and free-flowering fragrant variety with attractive apple green foliage.*

*For an unusual centerpiece, decorate your dinner table with water lily flowers floating in a shallow bowl of water.*

▶ *N. 'Rose Arey' has large, starlike flowers; a central boss of golden stamens; and an overpowering aniseed fragrance. It is a widely grown variety.*

# Large water lilies

When grown in sizable lakes and ponds, large water lilies are spectacular plants. The problem starts when they are planted in a small garden pond. In no time at all the leaves stick up out of the water and the plants cease flowering. All large water lilies require a planting depth of 15–36 in (38–90 cm) and will spread to over more than 8 ft (2.5 m) across. Flowers range in size from 6–10 in (15–25 cm) and are available in many colors.

◀ *Nymphaea alba, the common water lily in Europe, has large, green leaves and pure white flowers. It is very hardy and ideal for large, deep ponds.*

▼ *Nymphaea 'Escarboucle' produces deep carmine–red flowers and large round, green leaves. It is easy to grow.*

## TEMPTING BARGAINS

When looking down a plant list or around a garden center, you may see a number of water lilies offered at a lower price than the rest. These will usually belong to the large water lily group because they grow more quickly than the smaller forms. Unless you have a very large pond, avoid the temptation of a bargain, and buy the smaller, more expensive forms.

◀ N. 'Gladstoniana' is a vigorous-growing water lily with very large, pure white blossoms and a distinctive yellow, central cluster of stamens.

▼ N. 'Marliacea Carnea' is a strong-growing variety with pinkish white flowers that improve with the age of the plant. A stunning choice.

▲ N. 'Texas Dawn' is the best yellow water lily for a large pond. The flowers are flushed peach at the base and offset by large, red-speckled leaves.

▶ N. 'Charles de Meurville' has a long flowering period, producing large, plum-colored blossoms, tipped and streaked with white.

LARGE WATER LILIES

# Tropical water lilies

In a pond in a greenhouse maintained at a temperature above 64°F (18°C), it is possible to grow tropical water lilies. These include a number of species with blue flowers (a color not present in hardy types) and can be divided into day- and night-blooming varieties. Tropical varieties are larger than hardy lilies, with bigger, often more highly scented flowers, and certainly more profuse. Flower sizes as large as 10 in (25 cm) are common, and some have flowers 12 in (30 cm) across that are held 12 in (30 cm) above the water surface. These are spectacular plants. Position them where they will receive full sun during as much of the day as possible.

▲ N. 'A.O. Siebert' is a day-flowering lily with pink blooms that deepen in color toward the center. It does best in shallow water in full sun.

▲ The very dark cerise pink to red flowers of N. 'Haarstick' open at night and close by morning.

◀ N. 'Emily Grant Hutchings' is another night-blooming variety. Reddish pink flowers open as the sun sets and may stay open into the next morning on overcast days.

◀ N. *'Mrs George C. Hitchcock'* is a vigorous night-blooming variety that can produce flowers up to 14 in (35 cm) across. Pale pink blooms with a yellowing center are held high above the water surface.

▲ N. *'General Pershing'* is a day-blooming (sunrise to sunset) variety, with pink, scented flowers measuring up to 10 in (25 cm) across.

▲ N. *'Mrs Pring'* has pale yellow petals and bright golden yellow stamens.

▶ N. *'Tina'* has dark blue flowers, often with a purplish tinge at the base. It is a small lily, ideal for a patio pond.

TROPICAL WATER LILIES

# Deep water aquatics

Apart from water lilies, there is a range of handsome aquatic plants that require deep water for their successful cultivation. These are mostly grown alongside the water lilies in the central part of the pond. Being tolerant of partial shade and moving water, they are ideal for situations where water lilies will not grow. They provide shade, cover for fish, and the underwater stems so important for various forms of pond life.

*Deadhead the scented flowers of water hawthorn to encourage new blooms to develop.*

▲ *Water hawthorn (Aponogeton distachyos) flowers from late winter till autumn, with a break in midsummer. They are easy to grow.*

▶ *Spatterdock (Nuphar lutea) is a large deep water aquatic with thick oval leaves. Its bright yellow flowers are held well above the water surface.*

◀ N. *'Mrs George C. Hitchcock'* is a vigorous night-blooming variety that can produce flowers up to 14 in (35 cm) across. Pale pink blooms with a yellowing center are held high above the water surface.

▲ N. *'General Pershing'* is a day-blooming (sunrise to sunset) variety, with pink, scented flowers measuring up to 10 in (25 cm) across.

▲ N. *'Mrs Pring'* has pale yellow petals and bright golden yellow stamens.

▶ N. *'Tina'* has dark blue flowers, often with a purplish tinge at the base. It is a small lily, ideal for a patio pond.

# Deep water aquatics

water lilies, there is a range of handsome aquatic plants that require deep water for their successful cultivation. These are mostly grown alongside the water lilies in the central part of the pond. Being tolerant of partial shade and moving water, they are ideal for situations where water lilies will not grow. They provide shade, cover for fish, and the underwater stems so important for various forms of pond life.

Deadhead the scented flowers of water hawthorn to encourage new blooms to develop.

▲ *Water hawthorn (Aponogeton distachyos) flowers from late winter till autumn, with a break in midsummer. They are easy to grow.*

▶ *Spatterdock (Nuphar lutea) is a large deep water aquatic with thick oval leaves. Its bright yellow flowers are held well above the water surface.*

* *Orontium* and *Aponogeton* seed freely. Look out for the tiny seedlings as they float into the pond edge; collect them and float them in a bowl of water until they are large enough to pot and be submerged.

▼ *Once mature, golden club (Orontium aquaticum) produces masses of upright, pencil-like blossoms in bright gold and white, plus large spear-shaped leaves.*

▲ *Water fringe (Nymphoides peltata) is a pretty plant that spreads quickly. Do not allow it to cover too much of the pond surface; rake out as necessary.*

# Bog garden plants

Bog garden plants enjoy permanently damp conditions but will not tolerate standing in water, especially during the winter. Pondside planting complements the pond and helps to blend it into the garden by slowly graduating from bog plants to garden plants. Because the soil warms up more quickly than the water, bog plants are the first to grow and flower, thus adding interest to the pond before the water plants are ready to grow. By careful selection, they can extend the season of pondside interest.

▲ *At 6 ft (1.8 m) tall, goat's beard* (Aruncus dioicus) *is an imposing background plant.*

▲ Astilbe arendsii *hybrids occur in many colors. Height and spread depend on variety. They do well in partial shade.*

▶ *The nodding blooms of fritillarias appear in spring.*

◀ *Bowles' golden sedge* (Carex elata 'Aurea') *positively glows in sunlight, but also retains its color in shade.*

◀ *The umbrella plant (Darmera peltata) is a perennial with clusters of white to pale pink flowers that appear on white-haired stems in spring before the foliage starts to grow. Year-round interest is provided by the vivid autumn colors of the large, rounded leaves.*

▼ *Dropwort (Filipendula purpurea) produces large, reddish purple flowerheads from midsummer.*

BOG GARDEN PLANTS

▲ *The tubular flowers of Joe Pye weed (Eupatorium purpureum), a native North American perennial, attract butterflies from late summer to early autumn.*

▶ *Water avens (Geum rivale) has feathery foliage topped by bell-shaped flowers during late spring and early summer.*

# *Bog garden plants (continued)*

While flowering plants are the main attraction of a bog garden, foliage subjects make a major contribution. They not only provide a cool green foil for brightly colored bog plants but also convey a feeling of luxuriance associated with waterside vegetation.

▲ *Prickly rhubarb (Gunnera manicata) takes years to reach its full size of 8 ft (2.5 m). Smaller varieties are available.*

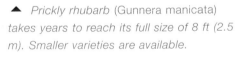

▲ *The day lily (Hemerocallis) has an extensive flowering period in summer. There are plenty of varieties in many colors.*

The flower spike on this young gunnera is already a prominent feature.

BOG GARDEN PLANTS

▲ Inula hookeri *is a vigorous plant with a mass of pale yellow, scented flowers in mid- to late summer.*

▶ *Hosta foliage colors range from green to blue, plus variegated forms. This variety is 'Blue Seer'.*

▼ *There are many beautiful varieties of the Siberian flag iris (Iris sibirica). This species does not require an acidic soil, unlike many other irises.*

▲ *This beardless Japanese iris (Iris ensata) produces stems supporting between three and fifteen flowers.*

# Bog garden plants (continued)

Some foliage bog garden plants add summer structure to the bog garden or streamside, notably the ornamental rhubarbs or rheums and stately ferns, such as *Osmunda regalis*, the royal fern. Much can be achieved with foliage plants by their careful placement, not only as complements to their flowering neighbors but also as architectural elements.

◀ *Golden rays* (Ligularia dentata) *has large, daisylike, flowers in mid- to late summer. The heart-shaped foliage may be attacked by slugs and snails.*

▼ *The leopard plant* (Ligularia stenocephala) *resembles golden rays, but the small, yellow flowers are borne on erect spikes.*

◀ Lobelia cardinalis *prefers a rich soil and bright, sunny aspect. It can be grown as a bog garden plant or as a marginal.*

▲ *Used as ground cover, creeping Jenny (Lysimachia nummularia) spreads into the water, blurring the edge of the pond liner.*

▼ *Spot-planted among flowering plants, ostrich feather fern (Matteuccia struthiopteris) adds contrast and interest.*

▲ *Purple loosestrife (Lythrum salicaria) has lovely flowers but is an invasive plant that is illegal in the United States.*

▼ *Royal fern (Osmunda regalis) prefers a shaded position, although it will tolerate sun. Provide very wet, lime-free soil.*

## Bog garden plants (continued)

bog garden plants, also sometimes described as moisture lovers, include
irable plants, both in terms of foliage and flowers. Ferns, hostas, and
sedges have very attractive foliage and can be used to really good effect, while astilbes,
irises, and primulas take some beating in terms of flower color.

▶ *Primulas are some of the first plants to flower in spring. This is* Primula beesiana.

▼ Primula japonica *'Postford White' is a reliable choice. It is easy to grow and it stays true from seed.*

◀ Primula vialii *has light green leaves. In late spring, red and pink flower spikes arise from the center of the plant.*

▶ *The scented, bell-shaped flowers of* Primula florindae *are held on tall stems.*

◀ *The flower stem of* Rodgersia pinnata *arches over hosta leaves in this pondside planting. The deep green foliage of the rodgersia is visible at the far left. Provide a shady site with protection from strong winds.*

BOG GARDEN PLANTS

▲ *The bright yellow blooms of the globe flower* (Trollius europaeus) *are held above deeply divided foliage on wiry stems. It can be grown in full sun or partial shade.*

▲ *Vivid* Schizostylis coccinea *will thrive in boggy conditions. Many colorful hybrids are available.*

▶ Spartina pectinata *'Aureomarginata' has yellow-striped leaves that turn orange-brown in late autumn.*

# *Picture credits*

PICTURE CREDITS

## Additional picture credits

The publishers would like to thank the following photographers for providing images, credited here by page number and position: T(Top), B(Bottom), C(Center), BL(Bottom Left), etc.

Dave Bevan: 29(TC), 48(BC), 49(TR, 49(BR), 51(T), 56(BR), 57(TL), 58(TR), 65(BR)

Eric Crichton: 6(TR), 10(BL), 62(BR), 63(TR), 64(T), 68(BR), 73(BL), 89(CL, CR), 92(BR), 93(BL, BR), 95(CR)

John Glover: 6(BL), 10(TR), 11(CL), 36(L), 38(TC), 84(BL), 85(CR), 86(CL), 88(TL), 91(BR)

S & O Mathews: 9(B), 37(BL), 66(R), 67(TR), 81(C), 86(BR), 87(T, B), 89(TL), 94(T), 95(BR)

Clive Nichols Garden Pictures: 38(TL), 80(BR), 91(TL, BL), 92(T), 94(CR)

Neil Sutherland © Interpet Publishing: 4(BR), 6(BR), 8(TL), 12, 14, 15(B), 27, 29(B), 49, 63(B), 35, 37(BR), 38(TR), 43(B), 45(B), 47, 58(TL), 61(TR), 62(BL), 63(TL, CR), 69(B), 72(R), 73(TL), 74(B), 76(TL, TR), 77(T), 77(BR), 78(TL, TR), 79(T, B), 80(C, BL), 81(TR, BR), 82(T, B), 83(T, CL, CR, B), 84(TL, TR), 85(T, CL, BR), 89(BR), 93(TR)

The Beaver Collection © Sue Westlake-Guy: 8(BR), 19(BL), 24, 36(C), 39(TR), 41(BR), 50(B), 54(TR), 56(TR), 57(TR), 60(TL, B), 62(TR), 64(BR), 65(BL, TR), 65(TL), 72(L), 73(TR), 74(T), 75(T, B), 76(B), 77(BL), 78(B), 80(T), 88(BR), 94(CL), 95(CL)